A SEA OF BLUEBELLS

MAURA O'GRADY

Swan Press

Published by Swan Press
32 Joy Street
Dublin 4

Copyright Maura O'Grady 2006

ISBN 0 9539205 8 5

Cover and illustrations by author.

Dedicated to my parents Henry and Mary K
and my brother Henry Jr.

Acknowledgements

Acknowledgements are due to the following publications: *Extended Wings* 3, 4, 5. *Quintet,* RI*POSTE, Reality Magazine,. Sailing Bread, Ireland's Eye, Seeing the Wood and the Trees* (eds. Rosemarie Rowley and John Haughton), *Western People, Mayo News, Modern Woman, Quantum Leap* (Scotland), *Moon* ((USA), *Labour of Love* (Canada), *Free Xpres Sion* (Australia), *Metverse Muse (*India), *Linkway Magazine* (England) and *Poetry for You Calendar.*

Some of these poems were read on: Anna Livia Radio, Dublin City University Radio and South Side Radio.

I would like to thank Christine Broe, Eithne Cavanagh and Mary Guckian for their help in editing, typing and proof reading these poems. Thanks are also due to all the members of Rathmines Writers for their encouragement and support over many years.

CONTENTS

The Silent Room	7
Gift from the Corporation	8
Three Dimensional View	10
November	11
Snow Fairies	12
The Big Snow 1947	13
Joan	15
The Monster Depression	18
The State of My Health	19
Ode to the New Glasses	20
Waiting for the 47	21
Raindrops	22
Guilty Aftermath	23
The Cherry Tree	24
Dipnosophist	25
Oscar	27
Our Hideaway	30
Attention Everybody	31
A Snail in the Boozer	32
Caterpillar	33
Lethe Waters	35
The Sea	36
Coming back from Saggart	37
Selenographer	38
Sundial Clock	39
Southampton L.1. 1956	40

Marooned	41
My Valentine	42
Waiting and Watching	43
Searching	44
Eclipse	45
Lunette Love	46
Welcome Home	47
Claidh Dubh	48
In Phillip's Fort	49
In a Far Off Time	51
The Poem	52
August Evening	53
Henry Junior's Bike	54
Image of Veronica	55
Dark Night	57
Sing Sing	58
The Leaf	59
Autumn	60
Waiting	61
The Wind of Change	62
Dream World	63
Whether or Not	64

The Silent Room

Velvet drapes a rich red
The plasterwork reminiscent
Of Victorian days
Through the Neo Gothic window
The moon silvers in
Leaving a gift of latticed light
The long table is cloaked
In a loose weave of tapestry
The quaint clock is silent
Its Roman numerals faded
In this secluded place
Bentwood chairs seem to beckon
We steal silently in
There's no climbing of stairs

Gift from the Corporation

On a dark night
In the depth of Winter
When I awake from a deep dream
I do not get a fright
For above the smoked stained marble
I find the street lamp's gift
An amber glow
Reflecting on antiquated jam jugs
And making a sunset of
'The Gap of Dunloe'.
In this warm atmosphere
I do not feel the winter's cold
Where night is richer than day
And my silver swan like magic
Has turned to gold
As I lie awake I do not fear
The night prowler.
I gaze at my portraits
Visible under the glow
Like an army of soldiers guarding me
They stand in a row.

Outside I hear the trickle of water
As an everun overflows
Then silence as it seeps into the wall
Making it damp.
I go back to sleep
Knowing I'm safe and cosy
Under the light of the tall street lamp.

Three Dimensional View

Gorse fires have broken out
On faraway Dublin Mountains.
Low cumulus clouds are gilt edged and purple.
Between tree tops, steady as a clamp of turf
Stands the Hell Fire Club.
(I wish a friend would call
I have a secret yearning for Fox's Pub)
And I can't see them from here,
But I know wild flowers grow aplenty up there.

In the cosy middle distance
Town houses snuggle among the trees
Out of the slate hanging, like square eyes
Their inset windows stare at me.
On brickwork of chimney stacks
A sinking sun leaves a warm glow.
In the lowlands, though hidden,
I know the dark Dodder weaves its way,

And here in the happy hinterland
On apex of palm
A blackbird sings his evensong to me.

November

In this muted month
Colours have waned
The sun has ceased to shine
I gaze at empty spaces
Dark evergreens are sparse
While stark branches
Wear a haunting look
Intricate tree shapes
Stand staunch
Iron silhouettes
Against a ghost grey sky
The wind whispers then howls
I lean against the force
I'm carried backwards
To rest between bleached stakes
Of barbed wire fence
I love these cold cleansing days
But tang of turf fire burning
Calls me to hurry home
To the comfort of an open fire

Snow Fairies

Without a Winter warning
You came one day in Spring
A horizontal hurricane
Sans a noisy zing
Snowflakes a brilliant white
Patchworked roofs and ground
You came fast and fluffy
You fell without a sound
You swept past my window
Whilst I was taking breakfast
You flew with such gusto
But I knew you wouldn't last
Suddenly you changed direction
As flakes turned to rain
And water poured straight down
My wishes all in vain

The Big Snow 1947

On that first day
A strong gale
Surrounded our house
Pushing powdery snow
Before it
Snatching the breath
Of anyone who dared
Out of doors

Indoors candles were lit
Light was blocked out
By the blizzard
Snow was frozen solid
Some drifts high as houses

We lived above fences
Boundaries wiped out
Stonewalls and hedges
Were non existent
We walked tall
We and the neighbours
Became one big family

On the second day
My father and brothers
Dug their way to the well
Our mother made sherbet ice cream
Placed in a fancy bowl
It was put out of doors to set
Under a galvanised bucket
In the freezing snow

Joan

She sat alone on the steps of the Bank of Ireland
Her bags beside one far reaching column
Weather beaten, bedraggled and sun tanned
I didn't disturb her as she sketched
But alas! I learned too late
That one can be over polite
For day passes quickly and too soon it's night

The next time I saw her she was praying
So I nodded and she smiled.
I'll see her again I heard myself saying
I didn't like to talk in church.
But alas! I learned too late
That one can be over polite
For day passes quickly and too soon it's night

No one knew who she was when she died
And she would have smiled I'm sure
Knowing someone had to decide
She has been reinterred and earth is all the same
Though paupers' plot has a new millennium name
But alas! For learning too late
I miss that ray of light
Day has passed too quickly – already it's night

Maybe at sunset her ghost will be seen
Sitting on the steps of the Bank of Ireland
Sketching a stylised sea-horse or a blue moon
clock
Lending character to College Green
Or what might be her attraction?
Angels making music in a floodlit fountain
Hewn from wood – a work in abstraction.

The Monster Depression

For years you taunted me
Haunted me
I lived in misery
You stabbed me with a knife
You took me over
Ruined my life
You followed me around
My days were in turmoil
But one day I stood my ground
'Go ahead kill me' I said
When I challenged you
Like a coward you stood back
Moved away, never made
Another attack.

The State of My Health

My blood pressure is high my insulin is low
I have a pain in my tum and a pain in my big toe.
When the doctor said 'Valetudinarian'
I though I'd get a heart attack
Then the specialist said 'Hypochondriac'
My suffering I don't have to explain -
It takes such long words to describe my pain.
People say I look very pale
Perhaps I need a long holiday
Drinking Buckfast Wine and good ale.
The other day I heard someone whisper
'Pain in the Neck'
Funny I didn't realise I had one there
Probably because I was suffering so much
With all the other pains everywhere.
Today I went to the chemists
I'm a little bit better now.
When I heard the price of the tablets
I got cured by the shock
The next time I have money
I think I'll buy a new frock.

Ode to the New Glasses

I see him but alas!
He hides behind two panes of glass,
A victim of presbyophia
Though happy in his framed Utopia.
He gazed at me as one unknown.
'He suffers from amnesia' I moan.
And while I stand and wait
He pretends to cogitate.
I look at him and sigh
But before I go I say 'goodbye'.
There's no response
From behind that window,
No turning of an eye
By way of innuendo.
Perhaps no vibrations
Pierced his inner ear.
The hammer missed the anvil
I fear, or could it be
An answer I don't deserve?
No, I diagnose paralysis
Of the twelfth cranial nerve.

Waiting for the 47

Outside the Metro Cinema I sit
In a colourful necklace of people
I am a blue bead
We half enclose the bronze porter
But he takes no heed.
We are waiting for our bus;
Over the Regal Inn near a porthole window
Pigeons too are waiting in a queue,
I peer at their seagreen wings
As they glide down to the cobblestones
Where welcoming children throw them bread
I like the camaraderie of other people
I overhear talk of faraway places
Where there is no rain,
Holidays in the Greek Isles
Or getting tanned in sunny Spain;
But I don't feel deprived
I'm happy with the cool breeze of Ireland –
Sorry folks! the 47 has arrived.

Raindrops

From a tilting wire
Where they were wont to be
Swallows now have flown
Only raindrops I see
Like crystals glistening in the light
They form an open necklace,
Some beads are still
Before dropping to the ground,
While others against gravity
Shuttle up hill,
Reminding me of people
Some are lost along the way,
Others fight on against the grain.
But I'm loath to read my own fortune
Hidden in a drop of rain.

Guilty Aftermath

In an open corner in the Monsignor's Garden it grew
Close to the footpath – this I knew
In the daylight I earmarked it for the night
At night I knew things would be quiet
So I walked down the road 'till I came close to the Church
Then in the dark I began to lurch
The lovely Laurustinus I found
Church property looking on to Holy Ground
With one eye on the presbytery
And one eye on passers-by
I cut its clusters clean
Then hid them and hoped I wasn't seen
But now on reflection –
I wonder if the Monsignor would have had any objection
Worse still, I didn't do it on impulse
I planned the crime
Thought it out, took my time.
Then armed with scissors off I went
And stole the flowers of the honeyed scent
Now when I pass by the Laurustinus Tree
I feel guilty when the bare patch I see
Bereft of its flowers –
Stolen by me!

The Cherry Tree

Was there method in his madness
An honest man he could not tell a lie
When asked who cut down the cherry tree
George promptly answered 'It was I'.

Was that tree just a delicate sapling
No blossoms reaching to the sky
Or a mature overgrown tree
Did the cherries hang too high.

Did George have a secret in mind
The cherry is a carver's tree
When he struck with the axe
He knew it was solid as could be.

I once read that the President had
A set of false teeth made of wood
Can't help wondering were they –
Ill fitting, very bad or 'cherry' good.

With that tree sprawling on the ground
The picture I am capturing
Makes me think he was perhaps
Going into dental manufacturing.

Dipnosophist

The *America* was floating along
There was chit chat and song
When he stepped out of the passenger list
To sit by me at table
A real dipnosaphist
A philosopher with
The right outlook on life
Relaxed and happy
He didn't believe in trouble or strife
He conversed in dramatic tones
With sometimes a sprinkling of French
An expert on every subject
But his big words I couldn't clinch.
A sort of connoisseur
Meticulous and cautious
I think he didn't know how to err
Sometimes he fell silent hand to forehead
Rodin's thinker
Then again he'd drop a clinker
Whether he told it in fact or fiction
His words he intoned
With perfect diction
He spoke with such verbosity
Ordinary words floated away
I was full of curiosity
Suddenly Triton lifted his fork
And the boat began to heave
We were miles away from Cork

Pegasus took to his wings
And the nine muses
Flew out port hole windows
And he forgot all his innuendos
Down to the bridge of his nose
Came his horn rimmed glasses
Then falling over
He swept the floor
With his long eyelashes
He lost his highbrow twang
Hit the deck with a bang
A doctor was called
Who sounded his back
I don't know if he was
A real doctor or a quack
But that dipnosophist
Certainly was cured
We passengers were all
Reassured
When out of his mouth
Fell an encyclopaedia of criticism
And the longest word in the dictionary
Antidisestablishmentarianism.

Oscar

Seen from the Mont Clare
You bring to mind
A summer's day.
You send me west
To a farmer resting
On a cock of hay.
But coming closer
To porcelain hands
Meissen face
I favour jade jacket
Though I expected
A bit of lace.
Flamboyant
Multicoloured
Pink collar, cuffs of pink
Speckled trousers
Shiny shoes
You sit on quartz plinth.
But, Oscar,
Where? Oh! Where
Is your shock of
Dark hair?
Your ringed hand
Holds a pretty rose
An admirer's largesse
I suppose!

Though you smile
Do I hear you sigh?
Over your head
Is that 'tint of blue
That prisoners call the sky'
Incarcerated
Behind railings
I thought you were free
But Oscar,
The gate is open
Otherwise I'd find the key.

Our Hideaway

Steps down from the busy street
I know a quaint and sequestered place
Where the black laths caress white walls
And arched doorways are low and deep set
Where pewter tankards have retired to high shelves
And old books are resting nearby
Where coach lamps glow
And dried flowers hang their pretty heads
Old pots and pans sit by the fire
While a sewing machine backstitches on the past
In this room of memories
We talk of old times and old ways
And when the music flows
On flagstone floor we tap our toes.

Attention Everybody
(Annie is not well)

I wonder if she lied
She drank the toxic
Ate the putrefied
Dozed off with
The electric blanket
Turned on
Got tangled in the clothes
Fell out of bed
Bruised her toes
Thought she was poisoned
Thought she got a cramp
Thought she hit her head
On the lamp
It was no joke
She wasn't paralysed but
She thought she got a stroke
Thought she got
An electric shock
Rang *Tallaght* at 3 o'clock *
The good doctor was consol'n
Measured both her feet
Said one was – indeed
Swollen
It's hard living alone
Today the receiver
Is hopping off the phone
     *Tallaght Hospital

A Snail in the Boozer

A porter bottle lay
On the ground
A few drops left within
Along came a snail
With its one foot
It slowly slid in
It didn't have to chew
Though a snail has lots of teeth
As many as twenty five thousand
It's true
It went on a drinking spree
Drank all the drops it found
But after that
It couldn't move
Was Boozer bound
Upending the bottle
We children let the snail
Slide out
It never moved again
But died a happy death
No doubt!

Caterpillar

You crawled a lot
Black streak with row of
Orange polka dot
I blocked your way
You played dead
A curled up cogwheel
I left you in
Your dandelion bed
Then shedding fear
You stretched a little
I returned to see
A new you
A lucky horseshoe
Brought you a nettle leaf
Thought you'd like a nip
Brought you a dew drop
Thought you'd like a sip
Unknown to me
You slipped away
But you'll come back
Another day
In camouflage
A pretty thing
An orange tip
With extended wing

Lethe Waters

Honey brick-backed houses,
Gothic chimney pots, trees,
A web of wires and dark slates
Casting a shadow on canal waters
Turning the surface to ebony
Where ivory swan is motionless
And tall reeds stand still.
In a dream
The wind played a tune on the wires
Ducks and moorhens awoke
And loomed out of rustling reeds
And on Lethe waters I sailed
With a floating swan –
And I sailed and sailed all night
Into the morning
Until that dream was gone.

The Sea

I feel the strength of the ocean
Tossing turning forever in motion

I hear the sound of the sea
White horses carry seashells to me

I see the colour sea green
That beautiful shade aquamarine

Summertime blue sky looks down
A colourful sea - waves just a frown

That's when you are really calm
You roll along a soothing balm

At night I picture you again
Sleepy now snowflake obsidian

With pale moon's reflection
A scene painted to perfection

Coming Back from Saggart

Followed by a muffed moon
We fly around cat's eye curves
We are going in the wrong direction
But we are not lost, just finding our way
At Rathcoole we will make a U turn
Double back on our thinking
I'm enjoying the fairyland lights
Green lights, up in the sky lights
Some fields star studded with lights
The sky is upside down, a mirage
Where cranes stand still.
Through tree branches we see city lights
Whole clusters of gold and bronze
We pass *The Red Cow* and *The Black Lion*
Somewhere along the way we lost the moon
But when I step out of the car
I find it's home before me.

Selenographer

I'm a selenographer
With the aid of my dictionary
I did the conferring myself
By nocturnal light each night
I study your physiognomy
Guessing, I place Arastarchus
Above the dexter dimple
I see no Cyclopes eye,
Akin to us creatures
You have two parted craters
Does your mouth hold Bailly
On dulia nights
I look for mock moon
Have found it once or twice
When I get my masters I'll spot
Whether your nose is Newton
Or not.

Sundial Clock

It's long hand was broken
It became a sort of sundial
She knew the time each hour
In her room no sun no gnomon
No shadow to show the seconds
No second hand but she learned
As the short hand snailed along
She followed its invisible trail
With index finger she gnomed out
From second to minute to hour
Where the long hand might lay
An expert when friends called
She read them the exact time
Before they glanced their watches
Left with no choice –
One becomes one's own gnomon

Southampton L.I. 1956

She clipped the treetops
Of the house next door
Then flew over our house
Me in my attic room
Face down on the floor
Muttering aspirations
In the night light
I saw the black silhouette
Flying low. Its pilot
A woman in a stolen jet
Unconcerned as a black crow
Her mind on Roma
She swerved before
Crash landing
Over in Ronconcoma

Marooned

Marooned outside a maroon door
I wait for maroon coloured car
To carry me over red bricked ramps
Through side streets and highways of tar
But I'm not alone as I look down
On sparkling granite steps
Over my head he has one eye on me
Though I'm not out of his depths
I feel his presence. I look up to see
That half face in the new half moon
I watch cars move over the back
Perhaps my friends will arrive soon
I see traffic lights change
From red to green, from green to red
Alone now he has slipped under a cloud
Deserted me gone to bed
Just playing hide-and-go-seek
He's out again though it's getting late
He shines down to tell me something -
Maroon colour car is at the gate.

My Valentine

On Valentine's Day
He came at night
He sent my present on ahead
Wrapped in meteorite
Then down he came
To chisel out my name
And to unwrap cohenite
And schreibersite
Such rare gems never found
On terrestrial ground
I fell in love
With this Martian man
From up above
Now I walk on air
Of gravity I'm unaware
And each time I hear a blip
I turn to see
A soundless spaceship

* Some rare minerals never found on earth are known only in meteorites, such as cohenite and schreibersite. Source: National Geographic Magazine.

Waiting and Watching

I stand at the window
I'm looking through lace
I have a creek in my neck
From watching your face
Part of you should be missing
It's time for an eclipse
Darkness is meant
To wipe out your chin and lips
But only little wisps of cloud
Blindfold your dark eyes
Gag your small mouth
Cause a distant disguise
The jigsaw is still intact
You are full faced and bright
Moon! Have I been watching
On the wrong night?

Searching

I didn't come to the window
To look for a Michaelmas Moon
Old Moore says tonight is not
A night for Clair de Lune
Since its pink glow has vanished
I didn't come to look for Mars
All I see are cumulus clouds
Though I came to look for stars.
Like sail boats they float
Across a clear night sky
Now I look for Leonid showers
I search and wonder why
Recently to this window
I made many late night trips
Alas! the weather was wet and dark
I didn't see the last eclipse
Has Temple Turtle moved near the sun
Have I missed the supernova
There are no stars to be seen
Not one – well – by Jove Ah!

Eclipse

She sits in a darkened room
Bathing her tired feet
In a stream of Aristarchus light.
She hopes no stratus cloud
Will invade the night
To obscure her view.
She marvels at astronomers
Who have pinpointed how soon
Gold will turn to copper
As she waits for eclipse
Of earth with harvest moon.

Lunette Love

My lunette love
I hold the key to your heart
You guard the secret
Of my velvet dreams.
Patiently you wait while I plan
Our next weekend
Away
Your tapestry jacket
A bit faded
From years of travelling
Still I love the rose pattern
We must go
For Christmas
I can see the two of us now
Running for the last bus
Lost in the rat race
Just you and me
Suitcase.

Welcome Home

I stepped off the Red Setter bus
From Dublin
Walked winter's road in the dark
Nearing home I heard
A two-in-one bark
I called out Sandy! Tricksy! as I bent
To drop my case
Knowing my voice
Already paws were on my face
I hugged each fluffy head
Off they chased in the driveway
Not waiting to hear a word I said
They shook the back kitchen door
Then raced out again
A second welcoming
As excitedly into my arms they tore.

Claidh Dubh

From the quarter land
of the Castle
In the ancient territory
Of Sliabh Lugha
From the Land of Lugh
From the Plain of the Yew
Ghosts at your back
You went without warning
Landmark of old
You have been levelled
Dark fence of the dark secrets
Your solid stones
Now sunk in soil
I close my eyes
To picture at your feet
Where they once grew
Cryptogams – ferns and mosses
Blooming brambles with
Little Veronica and Herb Robert
Peeping through
Wild winds descend
From Mullaghanoe
There's nowhere to shelter
From sleet and snow.

In Phillip's Fort

She edged her way through blackthorn
Into the solace of shrubs and trees
She remembers the large boulder
Almost overgrown with wild sorrel
Clasping smooth white branches
She peered through the hazel thicket
The Ox Mountains
Cut across the middle distance
Leaning forward she scanned the horizon
'Till she found –
The Holy Mountain of Croagh Patrick
With Nephin Beag clinging to Nephin Mór
Gradually she returned
To find herself standing on a stone
In Phillip's Fort
She could see clearly now
She went home
Leaving her troubles with the trees.

In a Far Off Time

In that remote place
Of green pastures
She lived in a world sublime
To inhale the scent of white clover
She sat deep in meadow grass
Where crops of buttercups grew
Their gold petals spilling over
When the West Wind blew.

She hungered after wood sorrel
And wild woodbine
She loved wild pansies
Violets and eglantine
She owned a sea of bluebells
Gathered Blessed Virgin flowers
Among such beauty and fragrance
She remembers Utopian hours.

In marshy land her Daddy waded
To pick for her the ragged robin
The memory never faded.

The Poem

No ripe berries to enrich
No sweet scented flowers
Nothing to click in place
No jewels to make it shine
No frills no bits of lace
Can't whip up a tune
No rhythm to make it flow
Nothing to raise the spirits
No colourful thoughts
To give it a glow
No inspiration –
I search for suitable words
I find only desperation
If only I could write
Something to intoxicate
Something uplifting
But wait – Apollo looks in
Inviting me out
I can't resist mythology
I abandon poem alas!
Please accept my apology -
To fine weather I raise my glass

August Evening

Scent of pineapple weed fills the air
A half circle of swallows
Swoop above rooftops
Suddenly change direction
Fly back to their ivy glad nests
In the old pine grove
I listen to their noisy chatter
Before they settle down for the night
As I watch, a vermilion sun
Slowly sinks below the 'Windy Gap'
A cat with her kittens
Play round a box hedge
I try to stroke shiny coats
They evade my efforts
But out from under a cart
In the hayshed
Comes our dog Spot to give me the paw.

Henry Junior's Bike

I remember the time
Uncle Tommy gave it to you
Your smile then
Bright as the Dynamo.

At quiet moments in my room
You free-wheel into my day dreams
Then pedal off to St. Nathy's.

Other times your head is bent
Beside the upturned bike
Spooning off the tyre

Dipping the pumped up tube
Looking for air bubbles
Listening for the sound.

Hanging on the outhouse wall
The rusty frame remains
Wheels missing, Dynamo intact
Its light long extinguished

I stand on an old chair
To touch the handlebars
The nearest I can get to you now.

Image of Veronica

We, halfway up
The heathery hill
Picking bilberries
And looking down.
It was easy
To find her
As she passed
Fairylike,
Between bog cotton
And butterflies
Between
Little groigs and
Long moor grass,
Between hillocks
And hollows.
Her hat high
On her head
A pyramid of rushes
Reaching
Way above herself
And the rigid rocks
Below us.

Her latest novelty
She wore it
With an air supreme
Then fairylike
She spoke

'When we go home
We will have –
Bilberries
With sugar and cream'

Dark Night

Late at night I look out
Backs of houses and trees
Have merged with the skyline
The world is a silhouette
Some drapes are half drawn
Making most windows lancet
Throwing out elongated light
In this fairyland
One large light looms out.
Its mullioned window
Divided into strips
Of perpendicular darkness
Giving it an ancient arbour look
When the wind blows
Leaves are transformed into people
As they dance up and down
Between the strips
Like revellers in the night
Bringing the arbour to life

Sing Sing

I held my breath
As it caught my eye
The dull drab building stood
On an acre of wilderness
Two or three storeys high
Neglected –
With broken panes of glass
It didn't look like
Anyone lived there
And from mud patches
On window-sills
Sprouted tall wisps
Of wilted grass.
Our train had come
To a halt.
A friend clutched my arm
I wondered why.
Then a chill
Went through my spine
As out of the hushed silence
I heard a woman sigh.
Most had travelled here
To bid farewell
To next of kin
Before they were led
To death
In the electric chair.

The Leaf

All that remains
Is a filigree of veins
Was it some sawfly's supper?
Or what rasping ribbon
Cut it like a drill?
Some small creature
Had its fill
I admire the artwork
Skeleton of a leaf
Light as a feather
I hold it in my hand
Before letting it loose
To sail around me
In a whirlwind of weather

Autumn

There's a hum in the forest
As Aelous holds his breath
Suddenly he breathes out
Tall trees shake their heads
A young man's hat flies off
Dead leaves arise to dance
A tango along the ground
A swish of colour as they swirl
Round a leaning Eucalyptus
But chestnuts half hidden
In withered grass stay put
Awaiting the touch of tiny hands

Waiting

Strong strap door, studded closed
Weather worn, ring knocker
Waits for the touch of a visitor's hand.

Corroded terracotta pot
Is sun faded. An ivy branch
Cradles drip moulding.

The garden needs weeding
But here in this neglected place
Flowers still flourish

An opening in latticed window
Inhales florescence –
And I see hope descending

As song birds fly into the garden
A woman and child cross
Over the broken gate.

The Wind of Change

The wind blew the Summer away
It plucked gold glazed petals
From buttercups
Sent them whirring upwards
Now half hidden
In long meadow grass
They settle sideways
But green battle maces
Have stayed put
Defying the wind's strength
And under thorn branches
Cushioned by velvet moss
Little Veronica and Herb Robert
Shelter from the breeze
A storm is brewing
I hear a low soughing
Among a quincunx of old trees.

Dream World

I walk through a mystical world
A strange land I have unfurled
Where skies are topaz blue
Where hills and hollows change hue.

I'm lost in a dream of shady trees
It's restful here my minds at ease
Where Harebell and Spring Gentian grow
Where the sun shines through with amber glow.

A mythical moon is on the rise
I'm amazed at its gigantic size
Now dark night is closing in
Little stars appear disappear again.

The sky is brush stroked with lavender cloud
Brown earth is black where men have ploughed.

Whether or Not

Whether the sky is
Blue or leaden grey
Whether it's veiled in mist
Day after day.

Whether there's a wintry wind
Snow, or any icy thaw
Whether it's frosty or not
She holds each day in awe

Whether it's Spring
Bursting in buds and bird song
It's a good day
She is happy to plod along.

Whether it's dressed
in Summer sunshine or flowers
Whether it's snappy cold
And drenched in showers.

Whether Autumn trees
Are covered in gold or rust
She loves each day God sends
In Him she puts her trust.